It is the biggest news of the year: people will be going to Mars!

Spiders From Outer Space

by
Mir Tamim Ansary

GLOBE FEARON
Pearson Learning Group

Project Editor: Brian Hawkes

Editorial Assistants: Jennifer Keezer, Jenna Thorsland

Art Supervision: Sharon Ferguson

Production Editor: Regina McAloney

Electronic Page Production: José López

Manufacturing Supervisor: Mark Cirillo

Cover Design: Sharon Ferguson

Illustrator: Ron Bell/S.I. International

ISBN 0-130-23286-6

Printed in the United States of America

5 6 7 8 9 10 11 12   05 04 03

1-800-321-3106
www.pearsonlearning.com

1. Nothing Can Go Wrong

All over Earth, people are looking at TV.

"This is it," says a man on the news. "This is the big day." Behind him, people can see the spaceship.

"Oh, yes," says a woman sitting in a truck stop. "The big day is here at last. This has to be the biggest news of the year."

"Of the year?" says a man next to her. "The biggest in years, I would say."

"In years?" says another man. "Try 100 years. Try 1000. People are going to land on Mars. Don't you know what that means? People are going to walk on another planet! It will be the first time ever!"

"I just hope they get back safe and sound," says the woman.

"Oh, of course they will," says the first man. "Our scientists are pretty careful. They know what they're doing. They have been working on this thing for years. What could go wrong?"

On the spaceship are: Donna, Mu Lan, Jake, and Tyrone. Right now, all of them are working hard. There is a lot to do before they take off.

Donna is the scientist. She will study Mars after they land. She will study the rocks and the gas around the planet. She will look for life of any kind.

Mu Lan will run the radio. She will talk to the team back on Earth.

Jake knows all about charts and star maps. He will keep the ship pointed in the right direction.

Then there is Tyrone Day. He is the computer man. Computers run the ship, and Tyrone runs the computers. Tyrone will drive the ship. That is what his job really comes down to.

Tyrone knows everything there is to know about computers. He can take a computer apart and put it back together. He can make a computer out of old parts. He can make one big computer out of two little ones. He can do just about anything with computers. He is good with other machines, too. If anything should break, Tyrone will fix it.

A voice now comes over the radio.

"*Mars One. Mars One.* Come in."

Mars One is the name of the spaceship.

"*Mars One* here," says Mu Lan. "We are ready to start."

"Everything is green on the ground," says the voice. "We can start to countdown any time."

"Start now," says Mu Lan. She gives Tyrone a look. He takes his place in front of the computers.

"OK," says the voice. "Here we go, then:

10, 9, 8—"

The ship starts to shake and make sounds. Jake looks over at Donna. She gives him a little smile as if to say: "Everything will be all right."

Then from the radio come the words:

"TAKE OFF!"

The ship moves—not fast at first. It does go up and up.

Then it starts to go faster. Up. Faster. Up. Faster. Faster. Up. Up! UP! Tyrone is working the machines. He has no time to look at the others. He can feel the ship getting hot. He could not stand up now, even if he wanted to. The ship is moving so fast that he feels sick.

Then he cannot see. He does not know how much more of this he can take. Just when he thinks he will pass out, he comes back to himself. He finds himself sitting by the window. He is looking out. He can see stars and a dark sky. The ship is going really fast. Then he cannot feel it moving anymore.

They have made it into outer space at last. Mu Lan is still talking to the people back on Earth. Tyrone gets up.

"Boy! That was hard," he says. "I don't ever want to go through that again."

Donna looks around. "Oh, I didn't think it was so bad. Anyway, we are off Earth now. We should have no more problems."

"I just hope you're right," says Jake.

"What do you mean by that?" asks Tyrone.

"Just what I said. I **hope** we will have no problems."

"Do you think we will?" asks Tyrone.

"Why should we?" says Donna. "What could go wrong?"

"Well, you can never tell," says Jake.

"I guess you have a point," says Tyrone. "There is always something, isn't there?"

Just then Mu Lan says into the radio: "*Mars One*, over and out." She turns the radio off. "I'm with Donna," she says. "Our scientists know what they are doing. They have worked out every last detail. What could go wrong?"

"We could hit a rock," says Jake.

"What?"

"A rock," he says. "You know—a rock. There are lots of them in outer space. Aren't there, Donna?" He turns to the scientist. "Tell them. It would not even have to be a big rock. Would it? A rock no bigger than a baseball could get in our way and—crash! That would be the end of us."

"Yes," says Donna. "That **could** happen. So could 100 other bad things. Your head could fall off, Jake. If that happened, you would be done for. What's the use of talk like that? It gets us scared over nothing. Let's wait till something bad **does** happen."

"See?" says Jake. He looks around at the others. "Donna is on my side. She thinks something bad **could** happen. My head could fall off."

Then they all start to laugh. The fact is, they all feel a little scared. Talking helps. So does laughing.

"No, but really," says Tyrone, "we should have no problems. It's like Donna says. Our scientists are pretty careful. Everything has been worked out, down to the last detail."

"That's right," says Jake. The smile is gone from his face. "Our team back on Earth thinks of everything. Nothing can go wrong. Can it?"

2. The First Problem

The ship has been out in space for two days. No one is scared anymore. They have a new problem now. They have nothing to do. They feel too pushed together. There isn't much room on the spaceship.

"Do you have to sit there?" Jake says to Donna. He gives her a mean look.

"Why not?" She throws the look right back at him. "You don't own this place. I have every right to sit anywhere I want."

"Kids, kids," says Mu Lan with a laugh. She is trying to get them to lighten up.

"Who are you to call us kids?" says Donna. "What gives you the right to talk down to us?"

"I didn't mean it that way!" Mu Lan cries.

Tyrone has said nothing so far. He is sitting in the darkest corner of the spaceship. He is caught up in what he's doing.

Donna goes back there to be with him. "I have had it with them," she says. "Talk and fight, day and night. I can't stand them! Yet, I like them, really. It's just that this ship is too small. How do you do it, Tyrone?"

"Do what?" He does not take his eyes off his computer.

"Put up with us? We are only two days into this trip, and already I feel like I want to go home. But you, Tyrone! Nothing seems to get to you. What do you know that we don't? How come you hardly ever say anything?"

"I have nothing to say," Tyrone answers. "Anyway, Donna, I have to keep my mind on this thing."

"What thing? What is this work you're doing now?"

"This is not work, Donna. I am playing a game."

"A game?" says Donna. "A computer game?"

"Yes, like the ones kids play down on Earth," Tyrone answers.

"You're just a big kid yourself, aren't you?" says Donna.

"Well, I do like computer games," says Tyrone. His hands are moving fast. Donna sees lights moving in the computer.

"What's going on?" she asks.

"Well, right now—" But just then something bad happens in the game. He cries out, "Oh!" Then he laughs and sits back. "Well, I lost. Really, you should try this game," he smiles. "It will keep your mind off other things, Donna."

"Maybe we should all try them," she says. "These games could save us." She calls to the other two. "Mu Lan! Jake! Come here. Look at what Tyrone has."

Mu Lan does not seem interested. "A computer. What about it?"

"It's not just a computer. Tyrone has some games here."

"I'm not into computer games," says Mu Lan.

"I am," says Jake. "Is this a good one? What is it?"

"I call it **Over the Mountain**," says Tyrone. "But if you don't like this one, I have others."

13

"What do you mean, **you call it**?" Donna asks. "Did you make it up?"

"Yes. That's one of the things I do," says Tyrone. "I make up computer games."

"You're a man of many parts," says Mu Lan.

"He's really just a big boy," says Donna. It's not hard to see that she likes Tyrone.

"There is a little boy in every man," says Jake. "Move over, Tyrone. I'll take a turn at this game. Show me how to play."

It does not take long for Jake to lose. He laughs and says, "I give up for now. Anyone else?"

"I'll try it," says Mu Lan.

Jake looks at Donna. "Help me out here, Donna. Didn't Mu Lan say she is not into computer games?"

"Yes, I did say that. I will try this game one time," says Mu Lan. "What else is there to do around here?"

When Mu Lan is done, Donna wants to play. But Mu Lan will not give up the computer. "One more time," she says. "I know I can win. Let me play just one more time." So Donna lets her play another game. After that game, Mu Lan still doesn't want to stop. "I was so close!" she says. "Let me play just one more time." The others will not hear of it. They make Mu Lan get out of the way and let Donna play. From then on, they all take turns. But Mu Lan is a problem every time she gets on the computer.

3. Something Is Wrong!

The days pass by. Each one is pretty much like the one before. At the start of each day, Jake looks at his star maps. Then he looks at the stars out the window. If the ship has gone a little off course, he tells Tyrone. Then Tyrone does what needs to be done. Every day Mu Lan talks to the team back on Earth.

"How are things?" they always ask.

"So far, so good," she always says.

Then they say, "Keep it up," or "good work," or something like that.

One day, Tyrone says, "Let's not call Earth today. Just for a laugh. They will think something has happened."

"What a bad idea!" says Mu Lan.

"I was just kidding," says Tyrone.

Just then Jake gives a little cry. Tyrone turns to look at him. "What?" he asks.

Jake does not answer. He is looking over his star maps. His face is dark.

"Don't do this to me." Tyrone goes up next to Jake. "Is something wrong or what?"

"I don't understand this at all," says Jake.

"What is it? What?"

"We were right on course. Now we are way off."

"Maybe you're getting a bad reading. Something may be wrong with your machines."

"No. The problem is not with my machines. Look out there." Jake points through the window. "Can't you tell? I can. After all these years, I have a pretty good feeling for the stars. They don't look right."

Tyrone gives a scared little laugh. "Don't look right! What does that mean? How could the stars look wrong?"

"They're not in the right places."

"How could the stars all move in the night?"

"**They** didn't," says Jake. "**We** did. We are way over in some other part of space. Let me try to tell you what I mean. Let's say you're looking at a house. If you look at it from one place, it looks one way. If you walk over to another place, it looks different. That's because you're looking at it from a different direction. Right? Well, that's how it is with the stars. They look different now than they did—too different. We must be looking at them from a different direction. That means we are in a different part of space. That, my friends, is bad news."

"What's the good news?" asks Donna.

Jake looks at her. "Who said anything about good news?"

Tyrone feels cold inside. "Do you really mean it? Has something really gone wrong?"

"Yes, just don't ask me what," says Jake, "and don't ask me how."

"Do you know where we are? Can you even tell us that?"

"We are on the other side of the sun. To get to Mars, we would have to go back the other way. We are a long way from Mars now, and it's even longer from here to Earth."

18

"How long?" says Mu Lan.

"It would take us weeks to get back to Earth," says Jake.

"How could that be?" cries Mu Lan. "We have only been gone a week."

"That's what I don't understand," says Jake. "Our ship could not have gone so far in so little time. We are just not fast enough. So how did we get from there to here?"

"How do we get back? That's my question," says Mu Lan.

"We have to start right away," says Tyrone. "Mu Lan, get Earth on the radio. Maybe they can tell us what has happened. I will turn the ship around."

Tyrone starts up the computers. Mu Lan gets to work with the radio. Donna stands next to Tyrone. She sees a look on his face that she does not like. "What?" she says.

"I can't turn the ship around," he says. "The computers don't work. Nothing works. Something has a hold on our ship. It is taking us somewhere. Can't you feel how it pulls? We are going somewhere, and we can't do a thing about it."

"What's that sound?" cries Jake.

"It's the radio," says Mu Lan. "I can't raise Earth. This sound is all I get."

The sound coming from the radio is not a voice. It is just a sound. If a car could laugh and cry, it would sound like this.

Jake says, "How about it, Donna—can I be scared now?"

"Yes," she answers. Her voice is small. "Now is a good time to be scared."

"Yes," says Donna. "Now is a good time to be scared."

4. Crash!

Then it happens—crash! Something hits the side of the ship. Everything rocks to one side. Tyrone knows he is going to fall. He can't stop himself. He and Mu Lan smash together.

"We are under attack," Donna cries out.

"From who?" screams Mu Lan.

"We can't fight back!" Jake sounds more mad than scared. "We have nothing to fight with. Oh, our scientists think of everything—don't they? Well, here is one thing they did not remember to pack! We are—helpless!"

Tyrone pulls himself to the window and looks out. Something big moves by. It moves too fast to see. Then a light hits Tyrone in the eyes. He puts his hands over his face. He can't remember ever feeling this bad. He falls down.

He hears the sound of someone crying. He wants to help. He moves around looking for whoever is crying. Then he hears the sound again. He knows who it is. It is he himself. The voice he hears is his own. The idea of it makes him scared. Next, Tyrone feels as if he is outside himself. He can see himself—and the others—down below. The ship is shaking this way and that. It is like a ball in the mouth of a dog. The four people fall all over the place. Tyrone starts to lose his hold on the window. The next time the ship shakes, he is thrown down. His head hits something hard. Then everything goes dark.

***

Tyrone opens his eyes. There is no sound. Nothing is moving. He turns to one side and sees Mu Lan. On the other side of her is Jake. But where is Donna?

Moving takes a lot out of him, but he turns over again. There, on his other side, he sees Donna. Her eyes are closed.

"Donna," he says.

Donna makes a sound. She is trying to say something. He gets his head closer to her.

"What happened?" she is saying. "Where—are—we?"

Tyrone tries to answer. But he finds it hard to talk. So he just shakes his head. He thinks about his body. How much harm has been done? Did anything break? As far as he can tell, the answer is no.

So then he does a hard thing. He sits up. His head feels like some kids are playing ball inside it. They are throwing the ball against the inside of his head. Crash! Crash!

"Oh—," Tyrone puts his hands against his head.

Donna says, "Are you all right, Tyrone?"

"I will be. I think. Give me time," he says. "How about you?"

"I seem to be OK. Did you pass out? I did." She, too, is sitting up now. She and Tyrone look around.

They are in a kind of box. The box has only three walls. Where the last wall should be is one big window. There is no glass in this window. It is just open, and through the hole they can see a room.

It is a big room—as big as 50 houses. Its walls look as if they are made of metal. Something is moving on the other side. Tyrone can't make out what it is. The other side of the big room is too faraway. The light is not good.

"Well, Donna. I know one thing," he says. "We are not on our spaceship anymore."

"We can't be back on Earth," she says.

"Did we land on some planet?" Tyrone asks. "Could we be on Mars?"

"We were not any place close to Mars, remember?" says Donna. "Jake was saying the stars looked wrong. We were in the wrong place. Then—the crash happened. The attack! I remember now! Something attacked our ship! Then—I don't know what happened."

"Our friends seem to be in a bad way. Are they alive?" Tyrone looks around.

"They look as if they're just out cold," says Donna.

"We all took some hard hits. They could be out for some time," says Tyrone. "What should we do?"

Donna points to the room outside their box. "One of us should go out there and call for help."

"I'll go," says Tyrone. He starts out. When he gets to the window, he hits against something. It is something he can't see. He falls back, feeling his head.

"What happened?" Donna runs over to Tyrone. When she gets close, she puts out her hand to feel where a window should be. She, too, feels something there.

"Boy!" she says. "This is really something, Tyrone. It looks as if there is nothing here—like it is just air. I can feel something. It feels as solid as rock. What could it be?"

"I guess it must be solid air," says Tyrone.

"Air can't be solid!" cries Donna.

"Yet—this air seems to be," says Tyrone.

"It doesn't break. You can't move it. You can't get through it," says Donna. "This is not just a room, Tyrone. Are you getting that feeling? We can't get out of this place. Someone has caught us and put us here. Someone means to keep us here."

"Someone?" says Tyrone.

Mu Lan starts to move. Donna says, "Careful, now, Mu Lan. Not too fast. How do you feel?"

Jake stands up. "What is this place? Where are we? Let's get out of here." He starts toward the window.

"No, Jake! Wait!" But Donna does not get the words out in time. Jake runs right into the solid air. "Oh! My head!" he cries out.

"I tried to tell you," says Donna. "There is some kind of wall there. We are caught in this box, my friends."

Just then the lights come up. Now they can see the other side of the room. They see a line of boxes. There must be as many as 30 of them. They look just like the box the four friends are in. Each one seems to be open in front. It may have solid air where glass should be.

Inside each box is a different kind of creature. One has a creature that looks like a dog. The next has a group of creatures that look like sharks with legs. Some boxes have only one creature. Some have many creatures. No other box has people.

Just then Tyrone hears something. He looks at Donna. She looks back at him. They pull back as if to hide. There is no place to hide. So they end up against the wall, just waiting.

5. Big Creatures

A door opens in the wall of solid metal. It opens where no door could be seen. A big creature comes through the door. It is a monster. No other word will do. It has a head as big as a truck. Its head comes to a point. On the point sits a dark red ball that must be an eye. The eye can turn in any direction. The creature has two long red feelers on each side of its head. At the end of each feeler is a hand. The body of this creature looks like a big red ball. It has eight legs—maybe more. Tyrone does not really have time to count. He only knows that the creature looks like a spider. When it moves, it moves really fast.

Behind it come more creatures. They all look just like the first one—only bigger. The door closes behind them, and after it closes, not even a crack can be seen. There is no way to tell a door was ever there.

"I don't like the looks of these creatures," says Mu Lan.

"Now, now," says Jake. "That one on the right would not make a bad boyfriend. I think he likes you, Mu Lan."

"Another time I would laugh," says Mu Lan. "Right now, I have to tell you, I'm scared."

"Who isn't?" says Jake. "Can't you hear my teeth?"

"What do you think is going on?" Mu Lan asks.

"I think they are here to see the show," says Jake.

"What show?" says Tyrone.

"Us," says Jake. "Don't you get it? What do we do with animals back on Earth? Think about it. Then look around. Just look at all the different animals they have caught. We are all in boxes."

"We are not animals," says Mu Lan. "We are people. We can think better than animals."

"They are coming right to us," Tyrone points out. "They don't seem interested in anyone else."

"Of course not. We are new," says Jake.

"I don't know," says Donna. "I think these

creatures may be scientists. They just have that look about them. After all, I am a scientist myself. One scientist can always tell another one. I think they may be here to study us."

"I hope you're right," says Mu Lan.

"I don't," says Jake. "I don't want them to be scientists. You know how scientists study animals."

"How?" says Mu Lan. Her voice shakes a little.

"They open them up to see what they have inside. These creatures may want to do the same to us."

"You really know how to make a guy feel better," says Tyrone. He turns to Donna. "Do you have any ideas?"

"Just one," she says. "We have to let them know that we are thinking creatures."

"How?" Tyrone asks.

"That I don't know."

"Don't call it an idea till you have that part worked out!" Jake sounds mad.

The biggest of the creatures comes up to the wall of solid air. It looks in at the people. Then it starts to talk.

That is, it starts to make sounds. Tyrone and his friends don't know if the creature is really talking. Maybe it is just making sounds. They look at one another. No one knows what to do. They wait.

The creature talks some more. It points two hands up and two hands down.

"It wants an answer," says Mu Lan.

"What's the question?" says Tyrone.

"I don't know. We had better say something. It's getting mad."

"All right," says Donna. "I'll do the talking for our side." She goes close to the creature. "What do you want with us?"

The creature stops making sounds. It looks at Donna. It points at her. Then it points at its own head. Then it makes more sounds.

Mu Lan cracks at this point—she just can't take any more. "Yes, you!" she cries out. "She's talking to you, you big insect! Who is your boss? Get him in here—right now!"

The creature looks around at the others of its kind. They make sounds at one another. Then one of them points a stick at the far wall. A door opens in that wall again. The creature races through. Its legs are going like mad. The door closes after it.

"Where is that one going?" Jake asks.

"I don't know," says Donna. "But I have a feeling we are about to find out. I hope you didn't make them mad, Mu Lan."

The creature comes back with a machine that looks like a big ring. It points a stick at the window that cannot be seen. Then the window must be gone—because it comes right through. The creature takes Donna by the head and pulls her up. She cries out, "Let me go! You big animal! Put me down!" By this time, the creature has pushed the ring right against her face. "Let me go!" Donna screams again. "Let me go!"

The monster does put her down then—but not in a careful way. It just lets her fall. Donna ends up on her back. Tyrone runs to her. "Are you OK?"

"I have had better days," she says. She lets Tyrone help her up. "What are they doing?"

The creatures are sitting around the ring-like thing. All of them are looking at it. Out of the ring comes a voice. It is the voice of Donna. "Let me go!" she screams. "You big animal! Put me down!"

The creatures like what they hear. They race around the ring like happy ants. Then one creature puts the ring over its head. The pointed part of its head goes through the hole. The eye of the creature sticks out. The creature starts to wave its arm the way Donna had done. The ring keeps screaming in her voice. "Let me go!" it screams. "You big animal! Put me down!"

It looks just as if the creature is doing the screaming.

The other creatures put out their hands. They all want to try the box. Each one takes a turn. Each one sticks its pointed head through the ring. Each one shakes its hand and points at the others. The box keeps screaming: "Let me go! You big animal! Put me down!"

"I don't get it," says Tyrone. "What are they doing?"

"They are playing that they are me," said Donna. "It looks like some kind of game."

"Could that really be?" says Tyrone. Just then, the creatures fall onto their backs. They rock from side to side, making a new kind of sound. Their voices ring out in that big room. "What are they doing now?" asks Tyrone.

"It looks like some kind of game," says Donna.

"Don't you get it? They are laughing," says Donna. Her face is a little red.

"That's good, isn't it?" says Mu Lan. "Creatures that laugh can't be all bad."

"If only they were laughing **with** us," says Donna. "I have the feeling they are laughing at us."

"Not us," says Jake. "You. They are laughing at you, Donna."

"Yes, at me," says Donna. "You may be next, Jake. Bad for one of us is bad for all of us."

Now all the creatures are walking around the room. All of them are laughing. The creature at the head of the line is screaming: "Let me go! Let me go!"

"Why, look!" says Tyrone. "It's not wearing the box. That one creature is saying the words itself. That creature can talk now."

"Boy! It gives me a turn," says Donna. "That insect sounds just like me!"

The monsters line up in front of the box. They look at the people inside. The big one says, "Let me go! You big animal! Put me down!"

"You can talk now?" says Jake.

"You can talk now?" says the creature.

"It says everything we do," says Tyrone.

"It says everything we do," says the monster.

"That's not really talking, you know!" Donna tells the monster.

"That's not really talking, you know!" the monster answers back.

Tyrone looks the creature right in its red eye. He says, "I am one sorry so-and-so. I should go stick my head in a hole."

The creature looks back at him. "I am one sorry so-and-so," it says. "I should go stick my head in a hole."

Tyrone can't help but laugh. His friends laugh, too. The creatures look at the people laughing. Then they look at one another. They don't know what is going on. That much Tyrone can tell. Will they guess that he and his friends are laughing at them? If so, will they get mad? Tyrone moves back a little, waiting for an attack.

But no attack comes. The creatures move away, talking to one another. One of them takes out that red stick and points it toward the wall. The same door opens in the same wall. The creatures walk through. The door closes.

Tyrone runs to the window of the box. He puts out his hand. The air is solid again. He and his friends still cannot get out.

6. Talking to the Monsters

The monsters come back. One of them gets a hold of Donna.

"Oh, no! Here we go again," she says.

"Let me go! You big animal!" says the creature. It has some kind of a machine. "Put me down!" it says to Donna. It puts the machine over her head. Another creature has come up behind Tyrone. It takes his hands. Tyrone can't move. He feels something coming down over his head. It is a machine like the one Donna is wearing. Tyrone fights to get away. But it's no use. The machine comes down and down till it's on. Only then does the creature let him go.

Tyrone turns to Donna. The machine is over her head, but her face and mouth can still be seen. She is still screaming. "Stop it. You let me go!"

The creature pushes her head to one side with its red feeler. It starts to make a sound. A change goes over the scientist's face. Her mouth falls open. Her eyes get big.

"What?" says Tyrone. "What is it, Donna?"

She doesn't answer him. But she doesn't look scared.

The creature is still making sounds.

Then it hits Tyrone: those are not just sounds. They are words. They are hard to understand at first. They are like words you would hear on a bad radio. But the sound gets better as time goes by. The words stand out more and more.

"Donna—" says Tyrone. "This machine over my head—"

"I know," she says. "It does the same thing for me. It turns their sounds into words. I can understand these creatures now."

"What are they saying?" Jake asks. Then he says, "Oh, wait. I see."

"Me, too," says Mu Lan.

"Well, well," says the creature. "Good day to you, little animals."

"We are not animals," says Mu Lan. "We are people!"

The creature laughs. "People—animals—they are all the same to me. What? What? All the same. What?"

"Why do you keep saying **what**?" Mu Lan cries.

"It's how we talk. What? Who is the head of this group?" The creature takes hold of Mu Lan. "Is it you, little man?"

"I'm not a man," says Mu Lan. "I'm a woman."

"Man. Woman. What? It's all the same," says the creature. "But a boss—that's different! What?" It puts Mu Lan down and gets its hands on Donna again. "I must find the boss. Is this your boss? What? This little man here?"

"She's not a man," says Tyrone. "She's a woman."

"Did I ask if this is a man or a woman? Did I? What? What? No." The creature shakes Donna up and down. "Is this your boss? Answer me! Fast!"

"It looks like one of us has got to be the boss," says Tyrone. "It may as well be me. Put her down," he tells the creature. "I'm the one you're looking for. My name is Tyrone. I head up this group. What do you want?"

"Not so fast," says Jake. "Who made you the boss, Tyrone?" He tells the creature: "I'm the boss around here, if anyone is. If you have something to say, say it to me."

"Hold on," says Mu Lan. "I don't want them to harm you, Jake. The team will never get home without you. If someone has to die, let it be me. Sit down, Tyrone. Don't get up, Jake. I will go with these creatures."

"We are not going to harm anyone," says the creature. "We must find the real boss. What?"

Donna says, "Friends! It's best if I go. I am a scientist. These creatures may be scientists, too. If so, maybe I can talk to them as one scientist to another. Maybe we can make friends. Then maybe I can get us out of here."

7. The Boss

Donna goes with the creatures. They take her through the door and into a hall. Two of the creatures go ahead of her. Two go behind. She could not run away if she wanted to. But she doesn't want to. Not yet, anyway. She wants to see where they will take her. She is scared, of course, but she's a scientist. As a scientist, she is interested in all this, too.

She and the creatures walk and walk. They turn one corner after another. At times, Donna thinks they are going down. At times, she thinks they are going up. At no time does she really know.

At last, they come to another wall of solid metal. The creatures point their red sticks at this wall. A door opens in it. Donna walks through it. She finds herself in another room.

It is even bigger than the room she came from. One wall of the new room is a window. Through the window, Donna sees darkness, and in that darkness are stars. It looks like space out there.

Then it hits Donna. She and her friends did not crash onto some planet. They are not on a planet at all. They are in a spaceship as big as a small planet.

Then she lets out a cry. There, ahead of her, is *Mars One*—her own spaceship. It looks so small in this big room! It looks like something a kid would play with. There is nothing inside it anymore. All the machines and things from the ship are outside it now. They are sitting on the ground next to the body of the ship.

There are lots of the red spider creatures in this room. Donna sees three of them sitting around next to *Mars One*. These three don't have much to do, it seems. Each one has a can. They are all drinking some kind of green liquid. Donna thinks they have been drinking for awhile. They do not look too clean. They are not careful with their drinks. They let the liquid fall all over.

Some of the creatures are looking through the parts from *Mars One*. These creatures have bags. They look like they are at a sale of used things.

One creature finds a TV. It can see itself in the glass. It makes a happy sound and puts the TV in its bag.

Another creature is looking at a metal machine part. It must not like what it sees. It throws the part away. The metal part hits the first creature on the head.

This creature turns and makes a mad sound. The two of them face off. They scream. Then they run toward each other. They crash together and start to fight. They break the TV and some other things. All the other creatures just look on and laugh. No one tries to stop the fight.

Donna thinks, "These are not scientists. This is some kind of a gang. It is a space gang."

She feels someone push her. It is the creature behind her. The creature says, "We need help with the things from your ship. They don't work. What? What? What? I guess they were not well-made. What? You have to fix them."

"What things?" She knows it is no use talking about science. This creature is not interested in ideas. It's interested only in money. She can see that now.

"This thing." The creature raises up a box.

"What is this for? What? What is it?"

"That is one of our radios," says Donna.

"It doesn't work," says the creature. "Make it work. Right now. What?"

"I can't," says Donna. "That's not what I do. I can't fix things."

"You're the boss. You are the head of your group."

"That's not the job of a boss. Not where I come from. A boss doesn't fix things," she tells them.

"Our boss does. He can fix anything. What? That's our boss." The creature points. Donna looks. She sees one of the creatures that has been drinking. Just as Donna looks, the "boss" falls over. Green liquid runs all over its head.

"It looks like your boss has had a little too much," Donna says.

"Our boss always has too much," the creature says—as if this is a good thing. "What a boss! What! What! Now, you fix the radio."

"I told you. I can't. Tyrone is the one who can fix anything."

"So **he** is your boss! Why didn't you say so? We

will get him. You come back with me. Back. What? Back."

The creature takes her arm. It pulls her into that long hall again. It takes her back to the room where her friends are waiting.

8. What to Do?

The creature gives Donna a push. She falls through the window. She hits the ground in front of her friends. The creature comes into the box after her. "Who is Tyrone? Stand up, Tyrone. What?"

"Me?" says Tyrone.

"Yes, you," says the creature. It gives Tyrone a long look. "I'll be back. What? For you. What?" Then it leaves.

Tyrone turns to Donna. "Are you OK? Was it bad? What did they do to you?"

"Nothing." Donna is sitting up already. "I'm OK. Really."

"Did you find out anything?" Mu Lan asks. "What did they mean about Tyrone? Why are they coming back for him?"

"Give her time," cries Tyrone. "She's been through a lot. Can't you see?"

"That's OK, Tyrone. I want to answer these questions," says Donna. "Did I find out things, you ask? Yes, I did. Bad things. First of all, these creatures are not scientists—far from it."

"What are they, then?" Jake wants to know.

"I would guess they are like a gang or something. They steal things. They fight."

"Did you find out anything about this planet?" says Jake. "Do you know where we are?"

"That's the other thing," says Donna. "We are not on any planet. We are in a spaceship."

"A spaceship!" says Tyrone. "How could that be? It's so big!"

"Yes, it's big all right," says Donna. "It's even bigger than you think. They have our spaceship in the other room. They took everything out of it. Can you believe that? They break things. They are like big, mean kids. Two of them were in a fight over something from our ship. I saw them break a computer right before my eyes. That's why they want you, Tyrone. They want you to fix some of our machines."

"Well," says Mu Lan, "it's up to you, Tyrone. When you get out there, you have to do something."

"Like what?" says Tyrone. "Have you got any ideas, Mu Lan?"

"Look for a way out of this ship," she says.

"What good would that do?" says Donna. "We are in outer space, remember? If we leave this ship, we will die. We can't fly out in *Mars One.* That thing will never fly again—believe me. The spider creatures have seen to that."

"Well," says Jake. "I guess we will have to fight. The first thing is to get out of this box. Try to steal that stick thing they have, Tyrone. The one that opens the door."

Mu Lan says, "I don't think we can fight these creatures and win. They look so mean. They are so big. If they're some kind of gang, they are used to fighting. We aren't."

"Maybe you aren't," says Jake. "I have been in a fight or two in my time. I am not just going to sit here and let them do anything they want to us. I say we should fight. If we lose, we lose. So what? It's better to go down fighting!"

"It's better not to go down—fighting or any other way," says Donna. "These monsters could do us in without even trying."

"What if we get the other creatures out?" Jake says. "Some of them look pretty mean. How about that big shark thing over there? Or the one with the head of a dog? The lot of us together could put up a pretty good fight. We could even win."

"Together? How do we know these other creatures will be on our side?" Donna asks.

"Why not?" says Jake. "We are all in the same boat. We have all been caught by these same spider creatures. The others can't like it any better than we do. Of course, they will be on our side."

"Till we win, maybe," says Tyrone. "**If** we win, I should say! After that, who knows? We may have to turn around and fight all these other creatures. We can't talk to them. We don't know if they're good or bad. We don't even know if they can think. Maybe they are just animals. How do we know they will not eat us? No, no. We can talk to the spider creatures, as you call them. That's a start."

"I'm with you," says Donna. "I think we can talk our way out of this. We just have to get these spider creatures on our side. That's our best hope. The way I see it, every living creature has feelings. We just have to get to their feelings—somehow."

"You mean—make them feel sorry for us?" Tyrone asks.

"Something like that. Yes. Try to get one creature over to the side. Talk to it one on one. Creature to creature. You know what I mean?"

"I'll try," says Tyrone. "Maybe it will work."

"Show it pictures of your family," Donna goes on. Maybe this creature has some, too. Maybe it is thinking about its kids. Who knows? That could be a way to get through to its feelings."

"Remember I'm not married!" says Tyrone. "I have no kids."

"You're not married? Oh, that's right." Donna gives Tyrone an interested little look. Then she looks away. So does he. "Well, that's all right," she goes on. "You were a kid yourself not so many years back. You have a mom, don't you? A dad?"

"Had," says Tyrone. "My mom is gone. Only my dad is still alive."

"Well, start with that," says Donna. "For all we know, this creature has just lost its mom. If so, play on that fact. Play on anything that comes up. Just get the creature to feel sorry for itself. If it does that, it may start to feel sorry for you next."

"It's a good idea," says Tyrone. "I don't have any pictures of my mom."

"I do," says Jake.

"Where did you get a picture of my mom?" says Tyrone.

"Not **your** mom!" says Jake. "I have a picture of my mom. Here." He gives Tyrone a picture. "You can just say this is your mom."

"Why don't you take these as well?" Mu Lan hands Tyrone the pictures. "These are Dan and little Mu Lan. My kids. You can say they are your kids."

"But—But—" Tyrone looks at the pictures. "These people don't look like me at all!"

"So what!" says Donna. "The spider creatures will never know. They can't even tell man from woman, when it comes to people. Take the pictures, Tyrone. They may help. You never know."

Just then the door opens in the metal wall. One of the spider creatures comes in. "Boss man!" it says. It points a feeler at Tyrone. "You come with me! What?"

9. The Big Fight

Tyrone goes with the spider creature. "Get to its feelings," he keeps thinking. "Make it sad. Talk about home and family." He has the pictures in his hand.

The creature takes him into the same room that Donna was in. "Fix this," he says. He points to the radio that came out of the spaceship.

Tyrone looks around. The parts from *Mars One* are now all over the place. The ship itself is in three parts. Tyrone sees two of the creatures on the ground. Each has a metal can in one hand. There is some kind of green liquid all over the place.

"What's wrong with them?" Tyrone asks.

"Nothing," says the creature. "They drink. They fall down. What's wrong with that? Fix the radio."

"I will," says Tyrone. "Say, I guess you want to call home on that radio. Where do you come from, anyway?"

"Never mind that," says the spider creature. "Fix. Fix. Fix."

"OK. OK. I'm going to start right now," says Tyrone. "Too bad my mom is not here. That woman could fix anything. You want to see a picture? Look. Here she is—"

The spider creature pushes the picture away. "Not interested in your mom," it says.

"Really? I'm interested in **your** mom," says Tyrone. "You would not happen to have a picture of her, would you? She must be one good-looking spider. I base this idea on your looks, of course."

"Fix fast, or I hit hard," says the creature.

Tyrone stops talking. "This is not working," he thinks. "I am not getting to it at all. What can I talk about next? Its dad? The good old days? Friends we no longer see?"

Just then Tyrone hears a sound. The ship starts to shake. The two creatures on the ground get up. They look like they were never sleeping. All the creatures in the room start to run around like ants. Tyrone can't tell what they are doing. Lights go on and off. Then a really big door opens. The creatures go running through the door. Tyrone runs after them. Then he remembers about the solid air. He closes his eyes. He's scared that he may run into some of it now. When he opens his eyes, he has made it through the door. He is in a hall. Then he makes his way into another room— a really big room.

In this room are many of the spider creatures. One wall of the room is the biggest window Tyrone has ever seen. Through this window, he sees stars and darkness. He knows he is looking at outer space.

Then he sees a spaceship in that darkness. It looks like a long box. Fire is coming out of its side. The fire comes right toward Tyrone. He throws his hands up in front of his face and his eyes. But the fire does not hit him. He feels nothing at all. He looks again. The fire has hit the window. It has not gone through. "I must be safe inside this spaceship," he thinks.

He knows, now, what is going on. This spaceship is under attack. Another spaceship has attacked the one Tyrone is in. Again, fire comes out of that other ship. This time, Tyrone's ship answers with fire of its own. Each ship shakes and rocks. They are moving closer to each other. They are so close now that Tyrone can see the big window in the other ship. He can even see the creatures in there. They look like spiders. Each one has a pointed head. They look just like the creatures on Tyrone's ship. But they are all green. The spider creatures on Tyrone's ship are red.

Tyrone can feel that his ship is moving fast now. So is the other one. They are coming together too fast. They are going to crash. It will be a bad crash. Tyrone thinks he could die when that window falls apart. He looks around for a place to hide. He sees a big machine of some kind. He doesn't know what it is. He thinks he may be safe from the glass window back there. So he throws himself behind the big machine. He waits.

He hears the crash. "There goes the window," he thinks. But where is the sound of glass hitting the walls?

He looks out from his hiding place. There is no glass on the ground. "Maybe the window was not made of glass," he thinks. "Maybe it was just solid air." He comes out to where he can see the window. It is not just smashed. It is gone. Where it used to be is open space. Tyrone's ship and the other one are right against each other. They are window to window. This makes for a kind of door between them. Tyrone could go through the hole and right into the other ship.

There is just one problem. Some mean-looking green spider creatures stand in that door. They are the creatures from the other ship. They are about to come onto Tyrone's ship. But they will not get in without a fight. The creatures from Tyrone's ship are waiting for them.

With a cry, the green creatures attack. The walls shake. The creatures are fighting hand to hand now. Tyrone is scared—and why not? He's like an ant on first base at a baseball game. "I better get out of the way," he thinks. Just then one of the creatures gets hit hard. It falls back. It comes down right next to Tyrone. A little closer and it would have smashed Tyrone. Is the creature still alive? Yes. It gets right up. It throws itself back into the fight.

At first, it looks as if the green creatures are going to win. The red creatures give ground. Then the fight turns. The red spider creatures push back. They fight their way into the other ship. Tyrone can see fire and light. Then the fight moves around a corner. He can't see the fighting anymore. He can still hear the screaming. He finds it hard to take. He knows these are not people. Yet, he feels for them even so. "After all," he thinks. "Every living creature has feelings."

Then even the sounds of fighting die away. Tyrone looks around the corner. He is all by himself. Is it safe to come out now? He thinks about it. He wants to. But he waits too long. Just then he hears someone or something coming back his way. He gets into his hiding place again.

10. Feelings

Crash! Into the room fall two creatures. They're fighting like dogs. One of them is red. The other is green. Tyrone wants the red one to win. He thinks of it as "his monster." In his mind, he screams, "Go, Big Red!"

He is happy to see the red creature trip the green one. As the green creature hits the ground, the red one takes out some kind of long stick. It starts to hit the green monster with this stick.

The green one fights back. It fights hard. In fact, it pulls an arm right out of the head of Tyrone's monster. Tyrone sees that arm fly away and hit the ground. But the red creature just moves the stick to its other hand and keeps hitting. Losing an arm means nothing to it.

Now the green creature has a hold of its head. This could be bad. Every living creature needs its head. The green creature pulls hard. Oh, no! It pulls the head right off the red creature and throws it away. With the head go the arms, of course. Tyrone sees the head land in the corner. The three arms on the head wave and wave.

Does this stop the red creature? Not at all. Tyrone has never seen a fight like this. The red monster will not die. It takes hold of that stick with two of its legs now. It keeps hitting. It doesn't seem to mind losing its head all that much.

The head is doing OK without the body. In fact, it is still calling out from the corner. "Hit hard! What? What? More to the right! Again!" the head screams. The pointed part turns, so that the eye can look this way and that.

The body does what the head says. At last the green creature stops screaming. It stops moving, too. It will never move again. The fight is over. The red monster has won.

The red creature stands up. How can it get along without a head? Tyrone doesn't know. The creature is feeling around the room. It is looking for its head. Tyrone moves back to hide himself better.

At last the creature finds its head. Then it sits down. It puts the head back onto its body. It turns the head to fix it in place. It looks around some more and finds its arm. It puts the arm back in place, too.

Next, it opens a small window in the front of its body. Tyrone can see right into the creature.

What he sees in there are machine parts. Only now does he understand—at last. These spider creatures are not really alive at all. They are just robots. They are just machines.

The creature turns around. "Yes, we are machines," it says. "But what do you mean **just**? Machines are better than living creatures any day."

"It can't be talking to me," thinks Tyrone. "It can't see me. It can't know that I am here."

"Of course, I know that you are there, people-man. I can hear you thinking!" the creature says. It has an oil can now. It is putting oil on its parts. "In fact, in your mind, you are just about to scream."

"You can hear me think?" says Tyrone.

"Of course," says the robot. It takes a long drink from the oil can. "Can't you hear others think? Oh, that's right. You're not a machine.

Well, there you are. It's just like I said. Machines are better. This just goes to show it. We can think better. We can move faster. What? What? We can hit hard. Oh, how hard we can hit! We can fix each other when we break. Then, of course, there is the best thing of all."

"What is that?" asks Tyrone.

"We have no feelings. No feelings at all. Oh, I tell you. It is good to be a machine!"

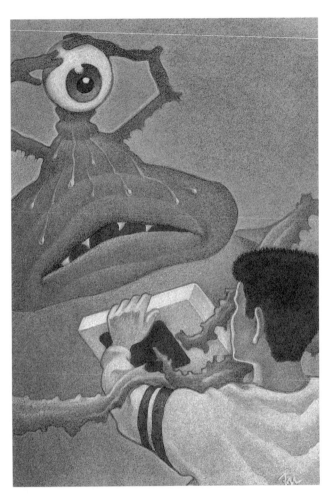

Now at last Tyrone knows: these creatures are not
alive. They are machines. They are robots.

11. Calling Earth

The creature pulls Tyrone out of his hiding place. "I will put you with the others for now. What? We have to clean up the ship. After that! What? You will fix the radio. Have you got that, man-boy?"

"Got it, Spider Thing," says Tyrone.

Tyrone's friends can hardly believe he's still alive. Mu Lan cries out his name. Jake says, "Man, it's good to see you!" Donna races up to him. She holds him without saying a word. (Tyrone likes that!)

"They did me no harm," he tells the others. "I didn't fix the radio yet. There was a big fight. Another spaceship attacked this one."

"Is that what happened?" says Donna. "We could hear that something was going on. We didn't know what it was. We were so scared!"

"Our side won," says Tyrone. "For what it's worth."

"Our side?" Donna gives him a look. "You mean the red spider creatures? Is that **our** side now?"

"The other ship had green spider creatures," Tyrone tells her. "Believe me, they were no better."

"Did you talk to any of **our** creatures?" asks Donna. "Did you get through to their feelings?"

"I have some bad news about that," says Tyrone. "They are not living creatures. They are robots. They have no feelings."

"Oh, no." Jake sits up. "They're machines?"

"Yes," says Tyrone. "They are machines, through and through."

"That's it," says Jake. "Turn out the lights. The ball game is over."

"Well, now! Just hold on! We are still alive," Donna points out. "Where there is life, there is hope."

"Donna is right," says Tyrone. "We can't give up. So what if they're machines? So what if they have no feelings? There must be an up side to this. There must be some way that people are better than machines. We just have to find it."

"I'll tell you one thing we have to do," says Mu Lan. "We have to get the word to Earth. We have to tell them there are other creatures out here. In fact, lots of them, it would seem. They need to know."

"How?" says Jake. "We can't even get out of this box."

"Tyrone is getting out. They will take him out there to fix the radio. When he goes, I'll go, too," says Mu Lan. "After all, they will need me to show them how to work the radio. While I am doing that, I will call Earth."

"I had better come, too," says Jake. "To call Earth, you will need to know where it is from here. Right? We will say I am needed, too. We can make up some story. Anything will do as long as they believe it. I will try to get a look at their sky charts when I am out there."

After awhile, the robot comes to get Tyrone. "I need these two to help me," says Tyrone. He points to Jake and Mu Lan. But he does not have to make up any kind of story. The robot just says, "OK." It is not scared to take three people along.

In the parts room, Tyrone gets to work on the radio. Jake asks to see a star map. The robot just says, "OK." It is not scared to show people its star map. It just points its stick to one wall. The wall lights up. That wall is nothing but one really big star map.

Jake studies the map. Then he tells Mu Lan, "We are here." He points to a circle of red light on the map. "Earth is over that way somewhere." He shows her a direction on the big map.

When Tyrone is done with the radio, Mu Lan gets to work. It does not take her long to get through. "Come in, *Mars One*," says a well-known voice. "Come in!" It is the head of the team back on Earth.

"Earth. This is Mu Lan. *Mars One.*"

"Mu Lan! What happened to you all? I can't tell you how happy I am to hear from you. Where have you been? We lost—"

Then the voice just stops. This throws Mu Lan. She looks up. She sees that the robots are doing something back behind the radio.

"What are they up to?" she asks Tyrone.

Just then Jake lets out a little cry. He is looking up at the star map. A red line starts to grow from the circle of red light. It moves in the direction of

Earth. After a time, it stops, and where it stops, another circle of red shows up.

"Why that must be Earth!" says Mu Lan.

"Yes," says Tyrone. "They wanted you to call Earth. Now we know why. They wanted to know where Earth is. Somehow the radio waves helped them work it out."

"What are you saying?" Mu Lan looks scared. "Do you mean that I helped them find Earth? Is that what you are saying?"

"Well—not just you," says Jake, "you and me together."

"But do they mean to harm—?" She stops. They all understand the question. No one gives Mu Lan an answer.

Tyrone's eyes are still on the robots. They have a TV from *Mars One*. The TV is working now. They are looking at it. In fact, they are getting a TV show from Earth. It is a game show. A man is saying to a woman. "What will it be? Will you take the $10,000, **or what is behind that door?**"

"Oh, Jared!" says the woman on TV. "I don't know! $10,000 is so much money, but—OK! I will do it, Jared. I will go for what's behind that door!"

The door opens. A car drives out. The woman screams and runs to put her hands on the car!

The robots like what they see. "This Earth looks like a good place," one robot says to another. "Look at all the things they have! Big cars! Houses! Food! Baseball! Money! CD players! Every kind of dog! There is so much to steal!"

"How right you are!" says Robot 2. "Next stop— Earth. We can go home after we hit this planet."

"Yes, yes! What, what! Earth will fix us up for a long time," says the other robot. "You know the first thing I'm going to do when we get there? I'm going to get a dog."

"A dog!" Mu Lan says, "What on Earth do you want with a dog?"

"Hot dogs are good to eat," says the robot. "There is nothing like a good hot dog. What? It said so, right on TV."

"That's it?" says Tyrone. "That's all you want from Earth? A hot dog?"

"No way," the robot laughs. "When we hit a place, we hit it hard. What?"

"Yes," says Robot 2. "When we steal, we steal everything. What?"

"Why leave anything behind?" cries Robot 1. "Steal it all, I say! Then throw away the things you don't want. That way you don't have to come back. You save time."

"That's right," laughs Robot 2. "That's what I always say, too. First, steal it. Then see if you want it."

"What you can't take—break," says the other robot. "That way no one else will get it. By the time we are done, Earth will be nothing but a rock."

"Nothing but a rock!" screams Robot 2. "Not one living thing will you find on Earth. Not one plant! Not one animal!" It laughs long and hard.

"After all," Robot 1 tells the people. "If a job is worth doing, it is worth doing right. That's what I always say. My dad was the same way."

"We are all going to die," says Jake.

12. Tyrone's Idea

Donna sees her friends coming back. "What's wrong!" she cries out. "You look so sad!"

Mu Lan tells her what has happened. Donna is sad, too.

"I did it," says Mu Lan. "I'm the one. I let these robots know where Earth is. Now the people back home are done for. Of all the ways for life on Earth to end! In an attack by a gang of robots from outer space—"

"There is no good way to die," Donna tells her in a kind voice.

"Don't be so hard on yourself," says Tyrone. "It was not you. It was I. I'm the one who did wrong. I should have told you. These creatures can hear us think. Right from the start, they could tell what we were up to. That's why that robot was happy to take all of us along. I should have told you."

"What if you had?" says Mu Lan. "Would that—"

Just then Tyrone sits up. "Wait," he says. "I have an idea. These creatures are machines, right?"

"Yes, of course. Robots."

"In every other way, they are like a gang of really bad kids. Right? They don't know right from wrong. They're not interested in ideas. They only want to have a good time. Isn't that right?"

"So it seems," says Donna. "What's the point?"

"Well—" Tyrone looks around at his friends. Then he says, "I have an idea. I'm not going to tell any of you what it is. Not yet. If you don't know, you can't think about it. If you can't think about it, you can't give it away. I'm just one guy. Maybe I can hide what is in my mind. This may be our only hope. Anyway, it's worth a try." Tyrone goes to the solid air window and calls out. "Robot monsters! Come here! I want to talk to you."

But no one comes.

"Maybe I can call them with my mind," says Tyrone. He sits down and closes his eyes. He lets ideas turn into words inside him. "I have something you want, robots. I have something you will like," he thinks.

The door opens. A robot comes running in. "Something I want? What is this thing? What? I want it now! Give it to me." It looks at Tyrone. Its red glass eye looks hot. "Will I really like it? What is it?"

"It's the best thing we had on our ship, and you're not even using it," Tyrone tells the robot. "Maybe you don't know what it is. Would you like me to show you this thing?"

"Yes. Show me this thing. What is this thing?" The robot sounds more than interested. "Can I sell it? Can I eat it? Can I hit someone with it? What is so good about this thing? Show me now. What?"

"Take me to that room with the parts from our spaceship. I will show you," says Tyrone.

The robot takes Tyrone to the parts room. Many robots are in there now. They are taking green robots apart as fast as they can. They are putting the parts into different boxes. Tyrone sees a box of hands, a box of legs, and so on.

"There it is," says Tyrone. He points to a computer from *Mars One.*

"That's a computer," says the robot. It laughs at Tyrone. "Little woman, we know all about computers. Don't you know that? We **are** computers."

"Well, that's not what I mean. I don't see any of you playing the computer games."

"Games?" The robot's face turns into a question. "What is a game?"

"See? You don't even know about it. A game is the best thing ever. Let me show you."

Tyrone sits down in front of his computer. He turns it on. He pulls up a game called **Over the Mountain** on the computer. He starts to play.

The robot stands there, looking. "What are you doing?"

"I am trying to get this little man over the mountain," says Tyrone.

"Why?" says the robot.

"That's just the point of the game. Don't ask why, or you'll never get it. Sit down and try."

The robot moves in front of the computer. It looks at Tyrone. It waits. Tyrone tells the robot how to play the game. He tells it about the little man. He shows the robot things to look out for.

"Don't fall into a hole—like this one," he says. "Keep away from monsters—see? There is one now. Oh, and look for food balls." He shows the robot what a food ball looks like. "Every time you eat one of these you can stand up to the monsters. But not for long," he tells the robot. "So look for food balls. Be careful."

The robot says, "Let me see. I eat a monster. Then a food ball comes after me—"

"No, no!" says Tyrone. Then he laughs. "Just get started," he says. "You will get it as you go along."

The robot starts to play. It is pretty good at the game. It moves the little man to the first part of the mountain. There it runs into a monster. The computer says, "You lose."

"I lose?" The robot looks mad.

"Yes, you can play again," says Tyrone. "Maybe you will do better next time."

The robot starts to play again. Another robot comes over. "What are you doing?" it asks.

"I am playing a game," says Robot 1.

"Game? What is a game?" asks Robot 2.

So Tyrone tells this new robot all about the game. Robot 2 stands for some time, just looking.

Then it starts trying to tell the first robot what to do. "No, no," it cries. "Don't go that way. What? Go the other way. What?"

"Don't talk to me!" the first robot screams. "Can't you see I'm playing? What? What?"

Just then a monster eats the little man in the game. The voice comes out of the computer again. "You lose," it says. "Is that the best you can do?"

"See what you made me do?" cries Robot 1.

"Me! I told you not to go that way," says Robot 2. "You should have done as I told you. You would have won. But no! You always think you know best! Well, now we can see that you don't. You don't know a thing. You are a no-good robot."

"Do you think you could better?" says Robot 1.

"Yes, of course. Much better," says Robot 2.

"Let's see you try. Sit down. Show us."

Robot 2 sits down. Tyrone thinks there is a smile on its face. (But with these robots it's hard to tell.) The robot starts to play. Right away the other robot starts to talk and scream. "Go this way. Go that way!"

"Will you stop it? Let me play!" Robot 2 cries out.

"No!" says Robot 1. "You did all that screaming when I was playing. Now I will do the same to you. Let's see how **you** like it."

"I said it before. I will say it again. You are one no-good robot."

"Say it just one more time," says Robot 1.

"You are a no-good robot."

Smash! Robot 1 hits Robot 2. The other robot hits back. Now they are fighting. The two big robots fall against the wall. They fall next to Tyrone. Tyrone has to move fast to get out of their way. The robots fall on the computer. The computer is smashed.

The robots stop fighting.

13. The Drug

"Now look what you have done," says Robot 2. "Can't you even say you're sorry?"

"Me?" cries Robot 1. "You did that! You. It makes me mad. I wanted that game. It was my game."

"Never mind," says Robot 2. "We will get more of these when we get to Earth, as many as we want."

"No. That's one thing you will not do," says Tyrone. "There are no more of these on Earth. I made this game. I am the only one who can make computer games."

The robots look at him. "Is that really so?"

"It's a fact," says Tyrone. He thinks the same thing in his mind. He thinks it as hard as he can. He knows these robots can read his mind. They are reading it now. He must not let them hear a different answer there.

After awhile, the robots look at each other. "It is really a fact," says Robot 2.

"We had better keep this guy alive," says Robot 1. "What?"

"What, what!" says Robot 2. "Give Game Man some food. Make Game Man happy."

"Make him happy? What's the use of that?" Robot 1 lets out a laugh. "Hit him! That's the only way to make an animal work. Don't you know anything?"

"But if you hit them, they die," says the other robot. "Then they don't work at all. You can't fix these creatures. When they die, they die for good."

"Yes, I know. Machines are better. I tell you, hitting is the one thing they understand. Here. Let me show you how it's done."

The robot comes toward Tyrone. It raises three of its hands. It is about to hit Tyrone. Tyrone cries out, "Wait! You don't have to hit me. I'll make you another game."

"You will?" the robots say in one voice.

"Yes. I want to help you. Didn't I say that? I will make not one, but two game computers. Then the two of you can play at the same time. I will need more parts. I know you have what I need somewhere on this ship."

"That we do, Game Man," say the robots. "Come." They take Tyrone to another room. There, they have things from many planets. Tyrone goes through the many boxes. He finds all the parts he needs and more. He sees other things as well. He tells himself those may be worth looking at some day. Right now, he has to make more computers.

He works hard. By the end of that day, he has made two new computers. The game is already inside these computers. The robots are happy. They start playing right away. Other robots come over to see what they are doing. Before long, they, too, want to play. They will not let Tyrone get any sleep. He must make more computers, so they can play right away. He makes more computers.

But even with more computers, the robots are fighting again. Now they all want to play. They need still more game computers. Tyrone says, "No need to fight. I can make all the game computers you want."

He makes so many computers that every robot on the ship has its own. The robots all start playing. They make little or no sound. The ship is still moving through the darkness of space. It is still moving toward Earth. But no robots are running the ship now. They are too caught up in their games. Even the boss of the robots is playing.

Tyrone looks into the game room. He sees one robot that can hardly move. That robot needs to oil itself. The oil can is not far away. But the robot does not go get it. It does not want to stop playing that long. It thinks it is about to win the game, so it wants to keep going. It just cannot pull itself away from the computer.

Tyrone can go anywhere in the ship now. There is no one to stop him. At last Tyrone makes up his mind to try something. He will steal the stick that can open any door or window on this ship. He goes up to Robot 1. He is scared at first, but the robot does not even look at him. Tyrone puts his hand out. He is as careful as can be. He takes the stick without making a sound. The robot just keeps playing. Well! Getting the stick was not even hard!

Tyrone uses the stick to let his friends out of the box.

Mu Lan says, "How did you do it? What happened to the robots?"

"Oh, they're still around," says Tyrone. "Come along and see for yourself."

He takes them to the computer game room. There is so much sound that the people can hardly hear each other. There must be 100 robots in there. But the sound is not coming from the robots. It is coming from their computers.

"What on Earth are they doing?" Donna asks.

Tyrone laughs. "They are playing computer games. I made a game for every one of them."

"Boy!" says Donna. "They really like computer games, don't they?"

"It is more than that," says Tyrone. "A lot more. Let me show you something."

He goes up to one of the robots. He takes hold of its computer. He starts to pull the computer away. The robot cries out, "No! Need computer— must have game."

"It's like a drug to them," Donna says.

"That's just it. Even to me these games are a little like a drug. I start playing, and I can't seem to stop. The robots are machines, just like the computers. To them, the games are even more like a drug. I had an idea this would happen. As you can see, I was right. These robots are not going anywhere. As long as we keep the games going, we have them. They are helpless, and you know what? I think the games are like a drug in another way. When people take a drug, they come to need it. They get sick without it. Yet, the drug makes them sick, too. They can't live with it, and they can't live without it. Right? Well, I think computer games are the same way for these robots. They can't stop playing. By the time we get to Earth, they will be done for. We can put them in boxes. We can have people pay money to come see them."

"That, and all the things on this ship—" Donna starts to say.

"Yes. Well, that belongs to the people of Earth. Our scientists will be so happy. There is so much new science on this ship it makes me laugh. The scientists on Earth will move light years ahead."

"How will we ever get back to Earth?" says Jake. "We can't put *Mars One* back together."

"Who needs *Mars One*?" says Tyrone. "This ship is already on its way to Earth. All we have to do is sit back and wait."

14. House of Robots

Years have gone by. Tyrone and Donna are taking a walk. Their little boy is walking between them. Little Tyrone holds his mom's hand. He is now four years old.

"I'm so happy we got married," says Donna.

"Me, too," says Tyrone.

"Me, too," says their little one. "Mom," he goes on, "can we go to the House of Robots? I want to see those monsters."

Donna looks at Tyrone. "What do you think?"

"Well," he says, "it's Saturday. We don't have anything else to do. But you know how it is over there. People are always after me. I get a little sick of it."

"Oh, yes. Everyone likes you. That is hard to take, isn't it?" Donna smiles.

"It's just that I didn't do it by myself," says Tyrone. "I only did my part. We all did—you, Jake, and Mu Lan."

"Jake and Mu Lan," says Donna. "You know, we have not seen those two in a long time. Why don't we call them up? Maybe they would like to meet us at the House of Robots. We could look at the robots together. After that, we could all go out and get something to eat."

"Are you kidding?" Tyrone looks at Donna. "Mu Lan is not on Earth. She has her own spaceship now. She's out in space somewhere, and Jake lives on Mars."

"Does he?" says Donna. "I didn't hear."

"Oh, yes. He has a talk show up there. I hear he's doing really well," says Tyrone.

"Good for him," says Donna. "But what kind of talk show does he have? I mean, what does he talk about?"

"Oh—all the things that could go wrong," says Tyrone. "All the bad things that could happen in the years ahead. That's what he talks about. Didn't you see his new book, **A Good Time to Be Scared**?"

"No. Does he have another book out? I read his first book, **Nothing to Smile About**."

"Well, this new book is more of the same," says Tyrone. "That's the idea behind his talk show, too. I guess people like to be scared. Lots of them call in, I hear. They talk about what bad things could happen."

"That sounds like Jake all right." Donna looks up at the sky. "He was like that even in the old days."

"The old days?" Tyrone laughs. "It has only been five years."

"I know. It just feels like 100," says Donna, "doesn't it? I guess that's just because of all the changes here on Earth. Well, anyway, let's go to the House of Robots."

At the House of Robots, there is a line of people. But Tyrone and his family don't have to wait in line. They go through a back door. All the robots are in one long hall. Each is in its own box. People can get pretty close to them. They can look at each robot through a window of solid air.

Solid air is one of many new things on Earth. People have these new things because of the robots they caught. Scientists took the robot spaceship apart. They did a careful study of the parts. In this way, they came to understand the science used by the robots. Now, science on Earth is way ahead of robot science.

What about the robots? Well, they just keep playing their computer games. As long as the games don't break, the robots are helpless. Their eyes are like glass. They can't stop playing. They win some, and they lose some. They never look away from their computers.

Tyrone stands looking at one big robot. Little Tyrone looks at it, too. A man and woman go by, hand in hand. The man says to the woman, "Look. Do you know who that guy is? That's Tyrone Day."

"Really? How do you know?" the woman says.

"I saw him on TV."

"Go talk to him," says the woman. "Ask him to write his name for me. Here, take my book."

Tyrone hears them. He says to Donna, "Let's move along."

Little Tyrone says, "Dad, how come those people know your name?"

Tyrone says, "It's called fame, little guy."

"How come you have fame?" asks the boy. "What did you ever do?"

"Not much," says Tyrone. "I just did my job."

"Oh!" Donna laughs. "Not much! He just saved Earth. That's all! You will read all about it when you get to school, Little Tyrone. You will read all about your dad in school."